Mindfulness Mastery:
Stepping into New Perspectives

Learn from Past Regrets, Live Presently and Plan for the Future.

Divya Parekh

Special Invitation

Visioning and Goal Charting to Success

SUCCESS is yours with the right VISION and GOALS. With this report: develop unique vision; think strategically over the long term; take small, measurable action steps that guide you to your vision, eliminate distractions and be focused on your purpose

Visioning and Goal Charting to Success

http://www.divyaparekh.com/product/visioning-and-goal-charting-knowing-the-dream-living-the-expedition-and-reaching-the-destination/

Or

http://bit.ly/1iV4Blj

$50.00 value DISC (Personality Style) and Hidden Motivators Assessment - COMPLIMENTARY FOR THE READERS ONLY

Achieve PRODUCTIVITY, PERSONAL and FINANCIAL SUCCESS in your life by: Understanding yourself. You are invited to take a complimentary Hidden Motivators Profile assessment (invitation code: 44voyage) because understanding yourself will help you maximize PRODUCTIVITY, PERSONAL and FINANCIAL SUCCESS when your MOTIVATORS are at work.

http://dpgroup.abeo.us/voyage/

CONTENTS

Perfection of character is this: to live each day as if it were your last, without frenzy, without apathy, without pretense.

Marcus Aurelius

Preface

Life constantly demands our attention, but when we become fixated on the past or worried about the future, we often miss vital information in our present situations. Cultivating a state where you are consistently aware of your present moment is not impossible, but it takes practice. Nevertheless, by learning to abide in the present, you acquire a sense of perspective that can allow you to learn from the past without it overwhelming you with resentment and regret, and plan for the future without it overwhelming you with anxiety or dejection. Implementing the guidelines in this module is the first step to changing your mental and emotional outlook to one that operates in the present moment.

In the beginner's mind there are many possibilities, but in the expert's mind, there are few.

Shunryu Suzuki

Chapter One: What Is Mindfulness?

People often confuse the concept of mindfulness with the idea
that one should "stop and smell the roses." However, if you
found yourself with your nose stuck deep into a flower in a field
where an angry bull was bearing down on you, this would be
the exact opposite of being mindful. Put simply, mindfulness is a
state of mind where you are fully conscious and engaged in the
present moment and with the demands of the present moment.

Buddhist Concept

The concept of mindfulness comes to us through the Buddhist
religion. The word "mindfulness" is one translation of the Pali
word *sati* (Sanskrit *smrti*). Other translations of this word
include "awareness" and "memory." Mindfulness is one's
capacity to avoid distraction from the present moment, but in
Buddhism it also means to avoid forgetting what one already
knows and to remember to do what one has an intention to do.

If mindfulness means avoiding distraction, what is it that
distracts us from the present? People are constantly besieged
with needs. Our basic needs such as food and shelter, and our
more complicated needs for love, respect, happiness, and so on
all compel us to consider our past and future in terms of what
to avoid and what to seek after. Consequently, the tempting
answer is to blame all the things going on in our world as the
source of distraction. A Buddhist would disagree. Instead of
everything that goes on "out there" being the source of
distraction, Buddhists blame what they call the "monkey mind."
The monkey mind refers to our own mental capacity to engage
internally in constant chatter. Sometimes internal mental

chatter can be helpful for working out problems, for analysis, and even for play. However constant mental chatter can also distract us from the things that are most important. And often, it can actually mislead us into misunderstanding a given situation. Buddhism teaches techniques in meditation to cultivate mindfulness and quiet the monkey mind.

Bare Attention

One aspect of mindfulness is the cultivation of bare attention. Bare attention is attention that is devoid of judgment or elaboration. Whenever we are faced with a new situation, we are tempted to try and consider what this new situation means to us. Will it be pleasant, scary, long lasting, or of minor importance? More often than not, we do not have enough information yet to make that assessment. When we start attempting to evaluate the situation before it has played out, this takes us into monkey mind style thinking, which often leads to distortion. One component of being mindful is to approach any present moment with our full and neutral attention.

Another way of thinking of bare attention is in the Zen Buddhist concept of "beginner's mind." To a Zen Buddhist, being a beginner is an ideal state because someone with no experience of something will also have developed no prejudice against it or other ways of placing limits on an experience. Since every moment of your life is unique, approaching each moment with innocence, as if you are a beginner and this is your first time experiencing this moment, allows you to keep yourself open to a host of possibilities that a more experienced person would either ignore or never consider.

Psychological Concept of Mindfulness

Although mindfulness originated as a Buddhist concept, psychologists from the 1970s to the present have studied the effects of Buddhist mindfulness meditation techniques and found that these are effective in reducing anxiety and reducing relapse rates in both depression and drug addiction. Recent studies have found that incorporating mindfulness into your life can increase positive emotions, improve the immune system, and reduce stress.

Despite the nearly universal agreement on the benefits of mindfulness, psychologists disagree on an exact definition of mindfulness or an exact method for developing mindfulness. Jon Kabat-Zinn , one of the first psychologists to study mindfulness as a secular concept, defines mindfulness as "paying attention, in a particular way, on purpose, in the present moment, and non-judgmentally." According to a later study, mindfulness studies in psychology tend to require two components for mindfulness:

- A quality of high attentiveness and concentration

- An attitude of curiosity and openness.

Memory

To this point, we have focused on just one aspect of mindfulness, that of bare attention in the immediate moment. However, as mentioned earlier, another translation of the word *sati* is memory, and there is a very good reason for this. Paying close attention to your immediate moment and environment sounds like a beneficial practice, and for the most part it is.

However, there are times where paying too much attention can be detrimental and force you into mistakes. If you have ever been told or told someone else not to over-think a situation, this is a good example where bare attention can be detrimental. In fact, a recent study has found that a mindful state can be detrimental for certain kinds of learning.

When you learn to ride a bicycle, for example, you pay less attention about the process and feel of yourself pedaling. Instead, much of the learning occurs subconsciously in what is known as muscle memory. Muscle memory is one example of a special kind of memory called implicit memory. This type of memory occurs through practice. For musicians who read music, for example, at a certain point in practice, they no longer consciously think about what the squiggles on the page actually mean. In fact, reading in general relies primarily on implicit memory. If you tried to be really mindful of what you were reading, by focusing on the shape of each letter or the makeup of each sentence, you would likely miss the overall meaning of a written passage, and it would take a long time to do it.

Mindfulness is helpful in tasks that make use of another kind of memory called explicit memory. This type of memory is helpful in learning new things and in memorization. However, when you wish to develop a habit, the combination of mindfulness when you are consciously willing yourself to do or notice something and scaling back your awareness as you allow the new task to be taken up in your unconscious mind through implicit memory is the ideal way to go.

Practical Illustration

Steve hated it whenever another driver cut him off. Usually he would get angry and without thinking about it, Steve would start honking his horn, flash his bright headlights, and drive up extremely close on the offending driver. Recently, Steve had begun to practice mindfulness. One day an elderly person in a Cadillac cut him off. For a split second he recognized how his thoughts had become angry and fearful at this point. Instead of reacting like he normally does, Steve decided instead to slow down and give the other driver a wide berth. He figured the other driver probably had not seen him, so he should change lanes and, as quickly as possible, get around the other driver, who may not be paying enough attention.

Between stimulus and response there's a space, in that space lies our power to choose our response, in our response lies our growth, our freedom.

Viktor Frankl

Chapter Two: Practicing Mindfulness

Mindfulness is a natural state of being. Throughout our lives we are frequently in this state without realizing it. If you have ever heard a noise at night and went to investigate, the level of attention that you bring to that situation is a good example of being mindful. However, we frequently divide our attention and, by necessity, we will selectively ignore aspects of our environment. When watching a sporting event on television, for example, a particularly enrapt fan might tune out conversation that is occurring around him or her in order to pay closer attention to the game. If the sports fanatics in this scenario consciously thought about paying attention to the conversations around them rather than the game on television, they could. In this sense, mindfulness is a mental skill that you can develop through practice.

Attention

When practicing mindfulness, whether through meditation or in a given moment, you want to pay attention to whatever comes up. For example, when you focus on your breath, note whether you are breathing in deeply or shallowly. Is your breath cold or warm? Fast or slow? Through your mouth or nose? If you feel pain somewhere, focus on that pain, note how it comes and goes or intensifies or subsides. You may notice aspects of breathing that you never have considered before. In fact whenever we are in any environment, we only pay conscious attention to a small number of details, typically.

Acceptance

When you meditate for mindfulness, or find yourself in a mindful state, it is important to accept things as they are without judgment. At some point, you may decide to act to change things, but initially you want to accept what you experience for what it is. Most religious thought includes some form of acceptance, whether it is the Christian view of surrendering your will to all God's will to be done, or the Islamic view that you must submit to Allah. By accepting things as they are, you allow yourself to remain open to a wider range of possibilities. So, for instance, when you meditate, do not do so with a goal in mind, as if you are trying to change yourself from one state to another. This may happen anyway, but that's a side effect. Instead, think of the meditation as an opportunity to observe how things change and how they don't change with the passage of time. Mindfulness is an act of observation rather than an attempt to change something. While you may determine later that a change is in order, initially you want to take a moment to observe how things are first.

Mindfulness Meditation

The best way to practice being mindful is through a regular program of meditation. Keep in mind that not all meditations are for the purpose of making you more mindful. Transcendental meditation and mantra meditation might increase mindfulness as a side effect, but these aim at an entirely different result. Furthermore, there are numerous methods of meditating that do aim at improved mindfulness. Some techniques take some time to learn. For example, Kabat-Zinn's Mindfulness Based Stress Reduction (MBSR) approach involves taking an eight week course where you go through guided meditations. This can get expensive and time consuming. However if you are interested in a self-directed version of Kabat-Zinn's course as an additional supplement to this course, you can follow the link at the bottom of this section.

The different approaches to mindfulness meditation typically focus on the following three attributes:

- Your body
- Your breath
- Your thoughts

This book provides a simple technique for mindfulness meditation. Spending approximately 10 to 15 minutes a day can help you dramatically improve your capacity for being mindful in any particular situation.

Scanning

One technique that Kabat-Zinn's approach to mindfulness meditation includes is called scanning, or body scanning. Once you are used to it, you can do it without the need for a guided meditation, but one option for beginners is to record your voice talking yourself through the body scan. You start by lying down on your back in a comfortable space. Focus your attention on the toes of your left foot and noting anything you observe. You then move your focus to the sole of your left foot, your heel, and the top of your left foot. Then you move your focus up your left leg – your ankle, your calf, your knee, your thigh, and finally your left hip. At this point, you do the same with your right foot and leg all the way up to your right hip. Once you have moved your focus up both legs, focus on your mid-section – pelvis, hips, groin, and buttocks – and then move your focus up your main torso – lower back, stomach, insides. At each point focus on how this part of you feels – are your muscles tense? Do you feel any pain, aches, coldness, warmth, etc.? Move your focus up the rest of your torso – your solar plexus, chest, breasts, spine, shoulder blades and shoulders. Once your focus has reached your shoulders, move your focus down the length of your left arm – your shoulder, bicep, elbow, forearm, hand, and fingers. Then do the same to your right arm. Finally we focus on the neck and head. Focus on your jaw, your cheeks and ears, eyes, forehead, back of the head, and finally top of the head. Once you have completed the scan, you can remain in this state for as long as you choose.

Practical Illustration

Alice and George both worked in the same, stressful department at work, the customer service center. When they started working there, they both dealt with extremely angry customers each day. While both found it stressful, they could handle it initially without it affecting their mood. Eventually, however, the negativity they dealt with each day began to seep into the rest of their lives. Alice had begun practicing meditation, but George did not. Even though her work was still often stressful, she learned to detach herself from the demands of angry customers. She realized that her customers weren't directly angry with her, and this helped to relieve her stress. George did not do anything to handle his stress. He just toughed it out. Eventually he got fed up and one day a customer called in and told George that his company and George himself were "woefully incompetent." George lost it and began curse out the customer before hanging up the phone. George quit his job the next day.

Your intellect may be confused, but your emotions
will never lie to you.

Roger Ebert

Chapter Three: Emotional Intelligence

While improving mindfulness is helpful as an intervention between our emotional cues and our reactions, it won't prevent us from feeling emotions or having angry thoughts at times. Nor is this desirable. In order to make effective use of the intervention that mindfulness provides, we need to better understand how we feel, why we feel, and what to do with those feelings. Psychologists use the term emotional intelligence to refer to this understanding.

The Purpose of Emotions

You may have heard it said that all emotions are valid. While this is true, it doesn't mean that you're well within your rights to throw a temper tantrum whenever you don't get what you want. The validity of emotions stems from the fact that emotions provide useful information about our internal and external environments. Imagine you lived in a time where giant saber-toothed tigers hunted human beings. Being able to feel and accept fear could mean the difference between dying as cat food or living to a ripe old age of 32. While these days the stakes are usually lower than being prey to some wild animal, when you feel an emotion, you need to pay close attention because that emotion is telling you something important.

High Performance Emotions

While all emotions are valid, and all emotions are helpful because they provide you with important information, some emotions help you to perform better at your work. These high performance emotions are enthusiasm, confidence, tenacity, and optimism. High performance emotions increase our arousal levels while still maintaining a wide and open focus. For example, when you are at your most enthusiastic, it's not uncommon for your thoughts to race. This indicates the high arousal and energy level involved in the high performance emotions. Keep in mind, however, that not every emotion with a high arousal level is helpful to performance. The other key factor that marks the high performance emotions is the wider focus and a sense of openness.

Swing Emotions

The swing emotions are called that because they can be either extremely useful in improving your situation, or they can actually help make a bad situation even worse. The swing element comes from how you choose to make use of these emotions. Swing emotions are there to tell us that something is not right in our environment. This can mean a whole range of things. The wrongness can reside in our thoughts about a situation or in the actual situation itself.

The swing emotions are anger, frustration, and anxiety. They are similar to the high performance emotions in that they involve high levels of arousal. When you are angry, anxious, or frustrated, your thoughts tend to race faster. A key difference between the high performance emotions and the swing emotions, however, has to do with your focus. When you are angry or frustrated, your focus narrows and you become blind to other possibilities.

The key to making swing emotions work in your favor is to identify the feeling and attempt to lower your arousal levels and widen your focus. As you can see, this is where being mindful becomes extremely useful. When you focus on your breath and your level of relaxation, you tend to open up more and slow down a little, and it's in this state of being where you can truly make the swing emotions work for you.

In the next two modules, we will examine some of the distorted thinking patterns that go along with emotions that narrow our focus, but first, something should be said specifically about the emotion of frustration. When you feel frustrated, this is a definite sign that something you are doing is not working. Because your focus is narrowed, you might even think that what you are doing is the only way to approach a problem. Here is a helpful phrase you can use to widen your focus and reframe an unsolvable problem into one with the possibility of resolution:

- The real problem is NOT _____. The real problem is _____.

This reframing of the problem allows you to open yourself up to a new range of possible solutions.

Blue Emotions

A third class of emotions is the blue emotions. These emotions are marked by low arousal levels as well as a narrowed focus. Blue emotions include dejection, depression, and disappointment. When you feel these emotions, it's a sign that you are low on energy and need to speed things up. This is why exercise is so often recommended for people suffering from chronic depression. Another way to address negative emotions is to widen your focus. Just like with the swing emotions, blue emotions often include distorted thinking styles. When you become mindful of these distorted thinking styles, you widen your focus. Calmness and mindfulness are examples of low arousal emotions with a wide and open focus, which are helpful for analysis and reflection.

Practical Illustration

Cedric had made plans earlier to meet some friends at the park after school. When he got home, he raced through his studies, which included preparing for a test the next day. Cedric was feeling pretty confident that he knew the material and would no doubt ace the test. Before Cedric could make it out the door, his father asked him to come give a hand with a problem that Cedric's dad was working on. Cedric's dad was trying to figure out how much material he'd need to install it along the line of the house's roof. "I forget, son," Cedric's father said, "how does the Pythagorean Theorem work again?" When Cedric began to draw a blank, he realized he wasn't nearly as prepared for the test as he had thought he was. He began to feel anxious about the test rather than feeling confident. Cedric decided to call his friends and tell them he wouldn't be able to meet them for at least another hour. He then went back to his room to study the Pythagorean Theorem.

The most dangerous of all falsehoods is a slightly distorted truth.

Gorge Christoph Lichtenberg

Chapter Four: Cognitive Distortion (I)

Whenever you feel emotionally ill at ease, it is completely natural for your thinking to become distorted as well. During high arousal periods when our thoughts race, we can make both logical and intuitional leaps that may or may not hold up when further examined. When our focus narrows, we close ourselves off to possible information and circle over the same types of destructive thoughts repeatedly. Cognitive psychologists refer to these as automatic thinking, which falls into various patterns. Using mindfulness to identify what our thoughts are doing helps us to make the necessary changes in our thinking which will allow us to improve the situation. These next two modules focus on various kinds of distorted thinking patterns.

Dichotomous Reasoning

Dichotomous reasoning means that you think in terms of hyperbole, extremes, and black and white. When you focus in on your thoughts, take note of whether you use words such as always, never, everyone, nobody, the best, the worst, or in terms of either/or etc. Rarely is a messy room or space the "worst you have ever seen" and no matter how rough a day you may be having, this doesn't mean that "everybody hates you." When someone you know makes a mistake, this does not mean that they are "pure evil" either.

Whenever you notice distorted thinking that involves dichotomous reasoning, try phrasing the thought in a complete sentence first. Automatic thoughts often come in the form of short hand words and phrases. The simple act of expanding these into complete sentences often reveals how absurd the thought really is. Take a few deep breaths and ask yourself, is it really the _____ (the worst, everybody, etc.). If you're being truly honest and open about the situation (i.e. mindful) chances are the answer is no. Try rephrasing the sentence to better reflect the reality of the situation. For example, "although it feels as if everyone is mad at me, in reality it is only (these specific people), and the reason why they are mad at me is …"

Magnification and Minimization

Typically people who magnify or minimize situations tend to gravitate towards one type of distortion. Magnification occurs when you blow things out of proportion. It's also often referred to as "making a mountain out of a molehill." Here are a couple of examples:

- "If I don't get that promotion, my life is over."
- "If that car gets into the lane before I do, I'm going to be late for work, and I'll get fired."

One particular form of magnification is called catastrophizing. This occurs when you give added weight to the worst possible scenario. Catastrophizing often includes an implied logical fallacy of the slippery slope, where one thing leads to another all the way to the worst possible disaster. Here's an example:

- "If I ask that girl out and she doesn't want to, and says no, she will make fun of me in front of everybody. I'll become the biggest laughing stock and everyone will know that I'm an absolute loser."

Of course, when you take into account the kind of short hand that goes along with automatic thinking, including magnification and catastrophizing, this type of thought, when you encounter it, looks more like this:

- "If I ask that girl out ... biggest laughing stock ... total loser."

This is what makes automatic thinking so insidious because between the ellipses, there's a whole bunch of logical leaps that don't actually follow logically.

If magnification is making a mountain out of a molehill, minimization is the exact opposite, making a molehill out of a mountain. Here are some examples:

- "It's okay if I miss work today. Nobody will notice, and I have plenty of absences to play with."
- "I know I cough a little bit from time to time, but it's not so bad that I have to quit smoking." (when the person has been coughing up phlegm and blood on a daily basis)

Filtering

Filtering occurs when you only hear the negative someone tells you, when their statement is a mixture of negative and positive. Here's an example:

- Your boss says: "I really enjoyed your presentation. You gave us a lot to think about. Some of it was pretty complicated. You also might want to shorten it, but I can tell you worked very hard on it, and I appreciate your dedication.
  You hear: "The presentation was too complicated and went on too long."

Another form of filtering is called disqualification. This occurs when you automatically discount something positive someone says to you as either an impossible statement, one made from naiveté, or one made for ulterior purposes. Here's an example:

- Your supervisor says: "Excellent work today on that project."
  You think to yourself, "She's just saying that so she can butter me up to work overtime."

Jumping to Conclusions

Another kind of distorted thinking pattern occurs when you draw a conclusion about what someone else thinks, feels, or will do in the future with little to no information. There are two additional kinds of sub-patterns that fall under jumping to conclusions: mind reading and fortune telling. Here are examples of both:

- Mind reading: you see your supervisor frowning and think, "She must be angry at me because I was two minutes late to work." Obviously, in this scenario, the supervisor may be frowning for reasons that have nothing whatsoever to do with you.

- Fortune telling: As a teacher, you are certain that a student will fail a test because she never comes to class. Although this might be a likely scenario, being certain of the student's failure assumes too much. She may be much better at studying at home and is entirely prepared for the test.

Another type of distorted thinking pattern that is similar to jumping to conclusions is overgeneralizing. When you overgeneralize, you base an entire class of circumstances on one singular example. For instance, if you went to a restaurant one time and had bad service, deciding that restaurant doesn't care about its customers would be an example of overgeneralization.

Practical Illustration

Mai's car broke down on her way to work one day. She felt overwhelmed and didn't want to think about getting to work or dealing with a mechanic. She considered taking a sick day. She thought to herself that it wouldn't be that big of a deal to miss one day of work. However, after thinking this, she began to feel anxious. She realized that today a district supervisor was coming and her boss Janelle needed all hands on deck. She called Janelle and told her about the situation and that she would take the subway into work, but she would be late. Janelle was silent for a long time. Mai assumed Janelle's silence was an angry silence. Mai began to apologize profusely but Janelle wouldn't say anything. Finally Janelle spoke, "Hey, Mai, are you there? Sorry to put you on hold. I was checking with my boss, and it turns out we'll be fine without you today, so take care of your car, and I'll see you tomorrow."

Problems cannot be solved by the same level of thinking that created them.

Albert Einstein

Chapter Five: Cognitive Distortion (II)

As you become more mindful and aware of your own distorted thinking in times of distress, you may notice your own tendency to fall into specific distorted thinking patterns more so than others. Before describing additional distorted thinking patterns, here are some steps you can take to address many different types of distorted thinking:

- Take a deep breath and be mindful of how you are thinking. Take note of whether your thoughts are coming in slowly or quickly. Are they coming in complete sentences or in phrases and shorthand? Are you using hyperbolic language in your thinking, words such as "always" or "never" or "everybody"? Are you using "I" statements or "you" statements? Are your thoughts specific or general?

- Rephrase your thought as a complete sentence.

- If you notice hyperbolic language, ask yourself if this is really the case. If you notice a lot of generalized statements, try to be specific. If you notice a lot of "you" statements, try to rephrase these as "I" statements.

Destructive Labeling

Destructive labeling occurs when you characterize something or someone in a generalized and negative fashion. For example, if you are a supervisor and an employee comes in late to work, thinking that this person is irresponsible or doesn't care about their job is an example of destructive labeling.

Destructive labeling can be applied to a situation as well. Perhaps you are engaged in a problem that you have not been able to resolve. You through up your hands and say to yourself, "this is stupid." By labeling the situation as stupid, you can give up on the problem, without remorse perhaps. However, the problem would still remain.

When you find yourself engaging in destructive labeling, a good way to counter the distorted thinking is to be specific. Rather than saying, "this is stupid," you can look at the specific issue and identify what is bothering you about it and why it is bothering you. When an employee is late, rather than characterizing the employee as irresponsible, rephrase the thought in a complete sentence that specifically and accurately addresses the situation. "When the employee was late this morning, I felt this behavior was irresponsible; however the employee may have a good reason for being late." Even if the employee did not have a good reason for being late and was acting irresponsibly, it's a lot easier to address an irresponsible action than an irresponsible person.

Personalizing

While this distorted thinking pattern can be similar to jumping to conclusions, it does so in a more specific way, by relating everything back to yourself or by taking responsibility for something over which you have no control. Here are two examples:

- When your child falls on the playground at school, you think, "This is my fault. I'm a bad parent."

- You call a friend and they don't answer or call you back. You think, "Why is (my friend) mad at me?" (This is actually an example of both personalizing, because you think your friend's reason for not calling is about you, and jumping to conclusions, because you don't know why your friend hasn't called you back)

Blaming

A similar distorted thinking pattern to personalizing is blaming. Whereas the personalizing distorted thinking pattern relates everything back to yourself, blaming occurs when you focus more on who you think is at fault in a situation rather than focusing on a resolution to the situation. When you cast blame, either at yourself or others, this rarely helps matters because it is more about identifying someone to punish than it is about finding a solution to a problem. When you find yourself casting blame on yourself or on others, try reframing the situation in terms that look for a solution. Ask yourself, "Regardless of who is at fault, what can I do to make this situation better?" Keep in mind that taking responsibility is different from taking blame. When someone is responsible, they are "able to respond," which means they are capable of changing a situation rather than being at fault in a situation.

The Tyranny of the Should

This distorted thinking pattern is also referred to as imperative thinking. This occurs when you fixate on how you think a person or situation should or shouldn't be, rather than how they or it is in actuality. This is another example where our thoughts about a situation are not helpful. For example, when you call someone and they don't call you back, you think, "(This person) should call me back." While this may be true, it does nothing to address the situation at hand, and it frequently points to an aspect of the situation or the other person over which you have no control. The pedestrian I almost hit when they started crossing the street SHOULD have looked both ways before they crossed the street. However they didn't and nothing I think or do will change that. Reminding yourself about how the situation is in actuality, what you have control over, and how you must adapt to the actual scenario are the best ways to counteract this distorted thinking.

Practical Illustration

James was usually a couple of minutes late to work every day, but occasionally he would be over twenty minutes late. One day when he was over an hour late, his supervisor Ginny had had enough. She thought to herself that his tardiness was her fault because she wasn't strict enough. Then she thought, "This isn't my fault. This is James's fault. He should be more responsible." Ginny was just thinking about how to punish James when she received an email from HR indicating that James had been in a serious wreck that morning and was in the hospital.

It may be necessary to stand on the outside
if one is to see things clearly.

Peter Hoeg

Chapter Six: Mindfulness Based Cognitive Therapy

Identifying distorted thoughts and counteracting them is one option for how you can choose your reaction to emotions. Typically, though, in order to have the wherewithal to identify an emotion or a distorted thinking pattern, you have to be in a place of calm already. While correcting a distorted notion with logic sounds simple, in practice it isn't always the most practical approach. An alternative to choosing a reaction to your emotions is to do nothing altogether. In order to do this, however, you have to get to a point where you see your "self" – the person you refer to when you say "I" – as separate from your thoughts and emotions. Mindfulness Based Cognitive Therapy (MBCT) seeks to foster this form of detachment, which has been vitally helpful for those who suffer from extreme anxiety in particular.

Mental Modes

Most forms of MBCT theorize that the mind operates with many subsystems. You have subsystems that constitute what you take in from your senses, for example. Most theorists agree that the two main subsystems or modes correspond with an emotional side and a logical side. The logical mode thinks verbally and is concerned with your sense of self. It can also be referred to as "cool" cognition. When your logical mode is dominant, you tend to be more reflective, calm, thoughtful, and less prone to action. When your emotional mode is dominant, you may think verbally to an extent, but you will also think in terms of images and a kind of verbal shorthand. The emotional mode is concerned more with relationships with others and is more prone to action. It can also be referred to as "hot" cognition.

Doing Mode

Another way of thinking of the two primary modes of cognition – emotional and logical – is in terms of action: a doing mode and a being mode. The doing mode is goal oriented and engages when you feel things aren't as they should be. Given the nature of arousal emotions, when these are present, you are goaded into the doing mode with a sense that you must do something in order to change your situation. Having goals and taking actions to reach them are worthwhile, but operating in a doing mode is not always helpful. Especially if you suspect that your assessment of a situation may be distorted. For example, when a parent disciplines a child from a place of anger, they are less able to consider the aims and consequences of their disciplinary practices than they would be able to if they did so from a place of calm.

Being Mode

Being mode, associated more with the logical mode of cognition, is not goal oriented. It is more interested in experiencing a situation as it is without a need to change anything. The various approaches to MBCT all concur that good mental health involves the ability of an individual to consciously switch between being and doing modes when appropriate, with the recognition that both modes are useful in certain situations and detrimental in others. For example, if you are crossing the street and a truck is barreling down upon you, operating in being mode will help to make your life a much shorter one than if you can switch immediately to doing mode and get out of the way.

Metacognitive Awareness

Mindfulness comes in handy in being able to consciously switch from being mode to doing mode or vice versa because it helps you to develop metacognitive awareness. This is a fancy word for saying you are aware of your thoughts and your thinking. The Buddhist term "detachment" is another good synonym for metacognitive awareness. When you can identify yourself as an observer of your thoughts and your emotions, the impetus to act on them is not as strong.

Practical Illustration

Marco and Sara had been dating for the past three years. One day, Sara noticed Marco looking at another woman when they were sitting outside a cafe. Sara felt her pulse and her thoughts begin to race. She thought to herself, "That cheating jerk!" Because both Marco and Sara had taken a meditation course recently and they had both been practicing mindfulness, Sara was able to pause and take note of her arousal. Instead of yelling at Marco for checking out another woman, Sara took deep breaths and allowed her anger to subside. She asked Marco if he thought the other girl was attractive. "Not as much as you are," Marco replied, "But I think I was in a class in college with her."

Be thankful for what you have; you'll end up having more. If you concentrate on what you don't have, you will never ever have enough.

Oprah Winfrey

Chapter Seven: Mindfulness and Gratitude

Becoming mindful of your mental and emotional states, logically counteracting your distortions in thinking, or detaching yourself from them – all of these approaches to handling emotions will reveal two fundamental truths about the emotions: first, they are transitory; and second, the "negative" emotions tend to attract the most attention. It is perfectly natural to notice and even fixate on the negative – all the things in your life or in others' lives that are going badly. The positive emotions, such as optimism and enthusiasm, they come and go, and frequently we take them for granted. There is a way to keep yourself oriented towards the positive, however, and being positively oriented is helpful in cultivating the high arousal, high performance emotions that can be the difference between a job that is tedious and a job that is rewarding. The secret is cultivating a sense of gratitude.

What is Gratitude?

Gratitude refers to that in our life for which we are grateful. This feeling of gratefulness can be extended to some source, and for religiously minded people this is often the case. However, you don't have to be religious to feel gratitude. The importance in this sense is more on how you feel, and how you are oriented than identifying the source of that gratitude. When we consistently focus on what is going well in our lives it keeps our outlook positive and fosters the high performance emotion of optimism.

Gratitude Journal

Oprah Winfrey once noted that the single most important thing she's ever done was to write five things that she's grateful for in a journal at the beginning of each day. And the science backs her up. Psychologists from the universities of California and Miami performed an experiment in 2003 that found that keeping a daily journal of what you're grateful for can increase your own sense of wellbeing throughout your life. This is a simple step that takes only a couple of minutes each day, but the effect is cumulative. It also doesn't matter how big or small the thing is when you make your list. Being grateful for a cup of coffee is just as significant as being grateful for your recovery from an illness because the important step here is to orient yourself to the things in your life for which you are happy.

An Exercise in Mindfulness and Gratitude

In addition to keeping a daily gratitude journal, there are other ways to cultivate an "attitude of gratitude." Here are steps for a simple exercise in gratitude that also incorporate the concept of mindfulness:

- Think of something for which you are NOT grateful.

- Once you have this thing that you are unhappy about in mind, be it a situation, person, place, or something else; now begin to focus on aspects of it that are good. If this is a person with whom you are unhappy, you can focus on traits about that person that you do like, traits that you are grateful for. If this is a situation, focus on the elements in that situation with which you are happy.

- If you have other areas in your life for which you are unhappy, try applying the previous two steps towards that situation.

- Try this exercise daily in addition to keeping a gratitude journal.

Forming a Habit

This training course involves incorporating certain activities into a daily practice. At this point, you have been encouraged to do the following things at least once a day:

- Mindfulness meditation for 10 to 20 minutes

- List five things for which you are grateful in your gratitude journal

- Focus on something for which you are ungrateful and note all of the aspects of it for which you are grateful.

While none of these activities are particularly difficult or time consuming, remembering to take time out of your busy day for them can be difficult. In order to do anything with regularity, we must make the activity into a habit. Here are some pointers on how to form habitual behavior:

- Use a reminder. For example, after you brush your teeth at night, use this as a cue to signal that it's time to meditate, or use the beginning of your workday before (or after) you clock in to act as a cue to list five things you're grateful for in a gratitude journal.

- Have a routine. Try to write in your gratitude journal or meditate at the same time every day.

- Reward yourself. Although developing mindfulness or a cumulative sense of gratitude are their own rewards, the act of setting up a specific reward helps to divide a large task into many small tasks. For example, for after a week of successively meditating, pick a small reward for yourself.

- Doing something consistently becomes automatic over time, but that time can vary between 18 and 254 days to do so. The average amount of time to make a habit automatic is around two months.

- If you miss a day, don't beat yourself up. Take note however why you missed it as well as any strategies to counteract whatever caused you to miss it. Be aware that a change in routine can disrupt habitual behavior and may require the development of a new reminder and routine.

Practical Illustration

Luz and Iris worked together at the same job. Initially, both engaged in bad habits. Luz smoked a pack of cigarettes every day, and Iris was addicted to sweets. During their training, they both decided to follow the course's advice and began keeping a daily gratitude journal. Luz didn't do her gratitude journal at the same time every day, but was more haphazard about it. After a week she had stopped. Iris on the other hand drank coffee every morning and decided to use making her coffee as her cue to write in her gratitude journal. When she asked her friend Luz how she was doing on her journal, Luz told her. Iris suggested that Luz try doing her journal at the same time each day by attaching it to another action that Luz did daily. Soon both were feeling more upbeat about life. They decided to get into the habit of working out together after work. As a result of this new habit, Luz decided to quit smoking, and Iris began to change her diet.

Optimism is the faith that leads to achievement. Nothing can be done without hope and confidence.

Hellen Keller

Chapter Eight: Cultivating the High Performance Emotions

As you become more mindful of your patterns of thinking and feeling, and as you become more grateful and positively oriented, you may note that when you approach a task with the right attitude, you tend to do better at that task. Although swing emotions such as anger and anxiety can motivate us to improve our circumstances, being able to incorporate emotions characterized both by high arousal and a wider focus will improve our performance in both our professional and personal lives.

The Emotion-Cognition-Behavior Triangle

All emotions have three components that work together, and you can think of them as a triangle:

- At the top of the triangle is cognition. The way you self-talk when angry is different from the way you self-talk when enthusiastic or when disappointed.

- At the bottom left corner is the arousal level of an emotion. Both high performance emotions and swing emotions are high arousal emotions whereas blue emotions dampen arousal. The arousal level allows emotions to act as cues to signal behavior.

- At the right corner is the behavior or reaction to an emotion. Mood management involves using cognition (your thoughts and assessment of a situation) to develop better strategies for reacting to your emotions.

Emotions also have a quality of being contagious. For example, when someone smiles at you, you feel an urge to smile back. When you feel underappreciated, this is a cue that you may not be appreciating yourself. Finding ways to increase your own enthusiasm and confidence makes you appreciate yourself more and this emotional state gets communicated to others.

Cultivating Enthusiasm

Enthusiasm is the get-up-and-go emotion. When you find yourself procrastinating, you are lacking enthusiasm. Military leaders and coaches of athletic teams understand that when their groups are collectively more enthusiastic, they will perform better. Thus, those famous war-time or half-time speeches really do play an important role. Here are some suggestions you can take to increase your own level of enthusiasm:

- If you have been practicing the activities in this course so far (mindfulness meditation, keeping a gratitude journal) you are actually well on your way towards increasing your feelings of enthusiasm.

- Celebrate every success, even the small ones.

- Listen to upbeat music that makes you happy.

- Engage in regular physical exercise.

- Surround your workspace with things that inspire and motivate you.

- At least once a day, enjoy a good laugh. In order to do this, you need to collect jokes and try to find the humor in situations whenever you can. Sometimes a favorite television show is a good opportunity to enjoy a deep belly laugh.

- Before you go to bed each night, write down on an index card three statements that will put you in a good mood, and place it on a nightstand or table so that you look at it when you wake up. This way you start out each day on a positive note.

Cultivating Confidence

Being confident is a delicate balance that many people have difficulty keeping. On the one hand, overconfidence can lead to arrogance that causes individuals to view themselves as better than or more important than other people. On the other hand, a lack of confidence causes self-doubt that will hinder creativity and can lead to blue emotions such as dejection and depression. Confidence is an arousal emotion where you believe in yourself and your abilities, and you can take steps to build confidence in yourself.

Steps to Creating Confidence:

- Trust yourself. Believe that you will be able to learn, grow, and accomplish your goals.

- Leave your comfort zone. Taking risks and trying new things will show you that you are capable of more than you realize.

- Accept praise. Be comfortable with well-deserved praise, but do not demand it. Refusing praise is not the same thing as humility.

- Be humble. Being humble sounds out of place on a list of ways to improve your confidence. We often mistake the concept of humility for humiliation, but they are separate. Being humble means we honestly recognize our limitations as well as our positive attributes. Being humble means you can understand where you need to improve and you are willing to learn.

Cultivating Tenacity

Tenacity is that sense that you are going to see something through no matter what. When we find ourselves confronted with large or difficult tasks, we often feel overwhelmed. This feeling of being overwhelmed can often lead to low arousal blue emotions such as dejection and depression, and it is precisely at such times when we need to cultivate the high arousal emotion of tenacity. So how do we do it? Here are some suggestions:

- Begin with the end in mind. Before you begin a task, understand what it is that you are doing, why you are doing, and what will it look like when you have successfully completed your task.

- Break a big job down into smaller and simpler jobs.

- Set goals and be sure to tell someone you trust about your goals. This puts you on the hook.

- Identify people who have achieved what you are trying to achieve and cultivate a relationship with them. How did they accomplish what you're trying to accomplish?

- Develop a timeline for your goals and strive to adhere to it.

- Remove distractions and use these as rewards for after you have accomplished your goals.

- Most importantly, don't let perfection become the enemy of progress. When we fail to reach a goal, it is natural to give up, but this is the most important time to keep going. Even if you didn't meet an initial goal, you probably are better off than when you started, and this needs to be celebrated.

Keep in mind that improving your enthusiasm and confidence levels also serves to improve your tenacity, so that all the suggestions in previous sections apply equally here as well.

Practical Illustration

Michael and Owen were both teammates on the varsity basketball team. They had a great season and made the playoffs, but during the final stretch before the playoffs, Owen injured his ankle. Both players knew that once the playoffs started, they would be about even against the other teams they were going up against in terms of talent. They would need to have Owen back at nearly full strength in order to stand a chance. What they also needed was to have an edge. Coach always told them that having a positive attitude can pay huge dividends. He would give speeches to inspire his players and increase their confidence. Michael decided he was going to do the same to help Owen get back to the team. He hung out with Owen during their workouts at the gym, and Michael was the first person to celebrate with Owen when the team doctor cleared Owen for practice. Meanwhile, Owen also realized that Michael would have to carry a bigger scoring load while Owen was out. He would show up at practice every day even though he couldn't play in order to encourage Michael and their teammates. "No one can stop you but you," Owen would shout to Michael after every shot Michael made in practice. After the first playoff game when Michael scored the game winning shot, the entire team stormed the court, including Owen who only had a slight limp. Michael credited his teammates, especially Owen, on helping him have the confidence to take and make that final shot. Both Michael's and Owen's enthusiasm and confidence were infectious and soon the entire team had a swagger, and this was just in time for Owen to make his playoff debut. Owen started off the game with a thunderous slam dunk that rattled the rim. The whole team realized at that moment that nobody could stop them but themselves.

The first step to exceeding your customer's expectations is to know those expectations.

Roy H. Williams

Chapter Nine: Mindfulness in Customer Service

Businesses can only be successful to the degree that they keep their customers happy. A single bad customer service experience can affect a business as drastically as numerous positive customer service experiences, so it's vital to approach these types of interactions with a clear and mindful focus and a positive outlook, even when it appears to be a difficult experience, especially then.

Individually Focused

When you work in a field where you interact with customers, it is important to prioritize, and your customer should be your highest priority. Regardless of your position in the company hierarchy, whether you're at the entry level or you're an executive, your customers are ultimately your boss, since without them, there's no company. Consequently, giving your customer your utmost attention in every interaction pays dividends. If customers sense that they are not being heard, they may go elsewhere. Whether you interact with customers in person or on the phone, it is important to eliminate distractions. Try to design the area where you interact with customers with this in mind.

Active Listening

The value of listening cannot be overestimated. However, listening involves more than simply hearing the words the customer says. Developing the skills of active listening makes sure that you not only hear the words your customers say, but that you understand your customers' concerns on a deeper level. Here are the different aspects of active listening:

- Use (minimal) encouragers. Encouragers are short words or phrases that indicate to a speaker that you are paying attention to what they are saying. Words, phrases, and sounds such as *Yes, Uh huh, Go on, Mmm, So what happened next?* etc. encourage speakers to continue speaking. It is possible to overdo this, and when you overdo it, you can give the impression that you are actually not listening, or, at the very least, you run the risk of disrupting communication through interruption.

- Repeat key phrases. This is another way to encourage speakers to continue and to make them feel heard. Here's an example: the speaker says, "Yesterday, I went to the store to buy a loaf of bread." The listener can combine a repetition of a key phrase with an encourager, "A loaf of bread. Okay, go on."

- Paraphrase and summarize the speaker's key points. *So what I'm hearing you say is ...*

- Offer empathy, but make sure it is genuine. *That must have been really tough* or *I can see why you would be angry.*

- Stay in the moment and listen fully. It might be tempting to interrupt because you've anticipated what else the customer is going to say. Keep in mind, however, that while you may have heard the same issue over and over from different customers, your interaction with this customer is **a unique experience with a unique individual.** Even if they say and do the same things exactly like what everyone else has throughout the day, they may need to fully articulate their experience in order to feel heard.

- Listening fully also involves taking note of volume and tone of voice and pace of speech. These indicate the emotional state of your customer. Higher volume, tone, and pace indicate an arousal emotion, enthusiasm, perhaps, but also anger, frustration, or anxiety. Context matters.

- Keeping a pen and pad of paper handy to write down any questions or thoughts you might have can counter the temptation to formulate a response as the speaker is talking. However, this can take you out of the immediate moment, and out of actually listening to the customer. Use this strategy sparingly when an issue is particularly complex. Think of it as taking notes on what the speaker is telling you.

- Probe with open ended questions. Open ended questions are the opposite of close-ended questions, which can be answered in a word. For example, *Were you able to login?* (close ended question with a yes/no answer) vs *When you entered your username and*

password and hit enter, what did the screen show?
(open ended question with a more involved answer).

- Be genuine. Active listening is not about using vocal and communication tricks to give the illusion that you care. Active listening means you are fully present in the interaction and that you truly care about what the customer is going through.

Building a Rapport

Active listening is only the first step towards building a rapport with your customer. A rapport is a state of harmony between you and another person or group. Here are some strategies towards building a rapport:

- Address the other person by name early, and reinforce that where appropriate. While addressing a person by name can come across awkwardly if overdone, too much in this case is better than not enough.

- Have a smile in your voice. When you smile as you speak, you insert a note of positivity into the interaction. However, a fake smile can communicate sarcasm instead, which brings us to our next point.

- Use "we" language to indicate the collaborative nature of the interaction. Remember that as a customer service representative, you are acting as a partner with your customer to find a solution to a problem.

- Employ (selectively) non-threatening ice breakers and small talk topics. Politics and religion are subjects to avoid. Remember that making small talk isn't always the best approach, especially if your customer sounds excessively angry or impatient.

- Be honest and genuine. If you truly do not know the answer to a question, be up front about that, but also demonstrate a willingness to find that answer. Using specifics helps.

- Speaking with an even pace and in a lower tone of voice helps to build a rapport.

- Be attentive to silence. Prolonged silence can be uncomfortable for some people, but a short silence allows you the opportunity to digest what the customer is telling you, and it indicates to customers that you are thinking about what they have said.

- Show agreement with the customer when you do genuinely agree, but after acknowledging agreement, express specifically why you agree.

- If you must disagree with a customer, give your reasons first before expressing disagreement.

- Be polite in your interactions. You can offer compliments, when genuine, but don't overdo it. Avoid offering criticism. Instead, offer alternatives in the form of a question: *What if we tried this …*

Timing

One of the most important aspects of a mindful approach to customer service is being aware of your customers' moods and expectations. This involves choosing the proper timing in your interactions. If a customer seems to be operating with high levels of arousal, taking the time to ask them about their day can horribly backfire. Conversely, if a customer seems perfectly content to interact with you socially and you rush to finish up your transaction with them, this can leave them feeling as if you don't value their patronage. The ancient Greeks had two words for time: chronos, which stood for chronological time or time as it plays out on a clock; and kairos, which stood for timing and the appropriateness for certain types of speech and action. It is this sense of time that is referred to here. Good timing means paying close attention to your customer's verbal and nonverbal communication to understand what type of approach is most appropriate.

Practical Illustration

Brian works at a cellular phone store in a shopping center. He enjoys chatting with his customers when they come in, and even relishes the challenge of turning an angry customer into a happy customer. Normally he will use an ice breaker to begin building a rapport with a customer. He smiles, and usually a customer will smile right back at him. One morning, a customer in a black suit comes in and says his phone stopped working, and he needs to get a loaner phone as soon as possible. He tells Brian that he called Brian's company's technical support number and they told him they would have a loaner phone available for him at this store. He introduces himself as Hermann. As Brian is looking up Hermann's information, he notices that Hermann is fidgeting a lot. He doesn't look at Brian, but instead keeps gazing at his watch. Normally Brian would try to start a conversation with Hermann while he pulls up the account information, but when he observes Hermann's body language, Brian decides this would not be the best approach. When he finally does get the account information up, Brian reads in the notes that Hermann's phone broke down right at the same time his mother died. Brian is really glad he paid attention to Hermann's body language and didn't try to break the ice with a joke. Instead, Brian hurries the interaction along and gets Hermann a replacement phone as quickly as possible. When Hermann asks what he owes them, Brian replies, "It's no charge. I'm really sorry for your loss." Hermann shakes Brian's hand firmly and thanks him while making eye contact. Brian can tell that Hermann is near tears. He can also tell that his own sensitivity in this interaction has made a customer for life.

Leaders who are mindful tend to be more effective in understanding and relating to others, and to motivating them toward shared goals.

William W. George

Chapter Ten: Mindfulness and Leadership

As you develop a greater awareness of the interplay of your thoughts and emotions, you will find that you have a leg up on your peers. Practicing mindfulness actually helps to make you a better leader, and modeling mindfulness for the rest of your co-workers helps to make your corporate culture a more positive and productive one. While the recommended approach to practicing mindfulness has been to engage in a mindfulness meditation for 10 to 20 minutes a day, this serves well as an introduction. To take your mindfulness practice to another level, engaging in two twenty minute meditation sessions daily is ideal. A mindful approach to leadership will enhance your mental toughness, increase your ability to focus selectively on that which you need to focus on, improve your capacity to feel compassion, and loosen the constraints we naturally place upon ourselves that inhibit our creativity. When studying these aspects of mindful leadership, it is important to remember that each concept overlaps and builds upon all the other concepts.

Mental Resilience

The United States Military Academy at West Point has recently developed a mindfulness approach to leadership training that focuses on enhancing mental resilience. The West Point model posits that the world has become increasingly volatile, uncertain, chaotic, and ambiguous (VUCA). Mental resilience is required in order to navigate a world marked by VUCA, but what is mental resilience and how can one develop it? Mental resilience is that quality which allows a leader to weather adversity, adapt to stressful situations, and recover. Mental resilience is mental toughness. Here are some approaches to increasing your mental resilience:

- Build strong social support networks. As a leader, you will frequently find yourself pulled in many directions. Developing a good network can help mitigate this, but keep in mind that this is a two-way street. Helping others can also have a positive impact on your own well-being as well as providing a strong network for the future.

- Approach crisis situations with both an immediate and long-term view. While you may feel a sense of impending catastrophe in the immediacy of a crisis, if you take a moment to imagine better circumstances in the future, this can help provide perspective.

- Act decisively. Once you have determined what needs to be done, take action. The more you procrastinate the greater the opportunity for problems to spiral out of control.

- Practice self-maintenance. When you are in a leadership position in particular, you will experience high degrees of stress. Using exercise, meditation, and relaxation to help ventilate that stress will allow you to perform better when the next inevitable crisis arrives.

Focus

While mindfulness is helpful in focusing your attention in a neutral and accepting fashion, as a leader, you will constantly find yourself having to decide upon what to focus. Understanding the goals and values of your company and your shared mission is a vital step towards prioritizing your focus. Familiarizing yourself with a company mission statement can help in this regards. Another helpful approach is to compose a personal mission statement, which focuses on your personal values, and a professional mission statement, which focuses on your leadership goals and values within the company. Familiarity with what is important to you and to your company can provide key insights as to which way to prioritize your focus.

Compassion

Developing a genuine sense of compassion for other people is a great side effect of a continuous practice of mindfulness. Compassion means that you try in good faith to understand where another person is coming from and the peculiar challenges that they have to face. Having compassion for others when you're in a leadership position is vital for building sustainable support networks. One helpful approach to leading others is to imagine your thought processes as transparent to everyone. When you do this, you become much more aware of negativity and instances where you are not being as fair and understanding as you can be. With a greater capacity for mindfulness, you can intervene in when your thoughts veer into the negative and reassess situations and people from a more neutral and accepting standpoint.

Creativity

The flexibility and adaptability that come with a practice of mindfulness are exceptionally helpful in being creative. Being a creative leader also means that you provide an environment where creativity is rewarded. Too rigid an approach to rules and regulations can stifle creative thinking, which requires the same openness and neutrality that you strive for in practicing mindfulness. In a stifled environment, the status quo tends to dominate, and the phenomenon of groupthink blinds you to your shortcomings. One approach to increasing your own and your team's creativity is to schedule times for play as a group. Keep in mind that this is play with a purpose – to help recharge the creative juices and allow them to flow.

Practical Illustration

Wendy had just been promoted to a supervisor position. Over the ensuing weeks her best friend Angela had grown more distant. Angela began showing up late to work on a regular basis. At first, it was just a couple of minutes, but eventually Angela would show up 20 minutes late or more. Wendy considered why Angela was showing up late. One thought that occurred to Wendy was that Angela was jealous, but she discarded that thought because she knew it wasn't fair to Angela. Wendy considered another possibility – Angela was afraid Wendy would change now that she was in a management position. Perhaps this was Angela's way of forcing a confrontation to determine how much Wendy had changed. Wendy considered that a possibility but she also wondered if Angela might be going through problems of her own that had nothing to do with Wendy. Even if Angela was worried that the nature of their working relationship had changed, Wendy couldn't dispute this because it had changed. Wendy wondered if she could still have a friendship with Angela outside of work. She decided to invite Angela to join her for drinks after work one day and ask her why she was always late. Wendy valued her friendship with Angela and wanted it to continue, but this new promotion was equally important to her. Wendy decided that if this promotion was the reason Angela was late all the time, then Wendy would ask Angela if she needed to change teams or ask her what other solutions they might arrive at together. If that wasn't the reason, then Wendy could find out why and work with Angela to help her.

We carry inside us the wonders we seek outside us.

Rumi

Closing Thoughts

- **Thích Nhất Hanh:** Walk as if you are kissing the Earth with your feet.

- **Amit Ray:** If you want to conquer the anxiety of life, live in the moment, live in the breath.

- **James Baraz:** Mindfulness is simply being aware of what is happening right now without wishing it were different; enjoying the pleasant without holding on when it changes (which it will); being with the unpleasant without fearing it will always be this way (which it won't).

- **Jon Kabat-Zinn:** You might be tempted to avoid the messiness of daily living for the tranquility of stillness and peacefulness. This of course would be an attachment to stillness, and like any other strong attachment, it leads to delusion. It arrests development and short-circuits the cultivation of wisdom.

Visioning and Goal Charting to Success

SUCCESS is yours with the right VISION and GOALS. With this report: develop unique vision; think strategically over the long term; take small, measurable action steps that guide you to your vision, eliminate distractions and be focused on your purpose

Visioning and Goal Charting to Success

http://www.divyaparekh.com/product/visioning-and-goal-charting-knowing-the-dream-living-the-expedition-and-reaching-the-destination/

Or

http://bit.ly/1iV4Blj

$50.00 value DISC (Personality Style) and Hidden Motivators Assessment - COMPLIMENTARY FOR THE READERS ONLY

Achieve PRODUCTIVITY, PERSONAL and FINANCIAL SUCCESS in your life by: Understanding yourself. You are invited to take a complimentary Hidden Motivators Profile assessment (invitation code: 44voyage) because understanding yourself will help you maximize PRODUCTIVITY, PERSONAL and FINANCIAL SUCCESS when your MOTIVATORS are at work.

http://dpgroup.abeo.us/voyage/